The Outer Bands

THE ANDRÉS MONTOYA POETRY PRIZE

2004, *Pity the Drowned Horses*, Sheryl Luna
Final Judge: Robert Vasquez

2006, *The Outer Bands*, Gabriel Gomez
Final Judge: Valerie Martínez

The Andrés Montoya Poetry Prize,
named after the late California native and author of
the award-winning book, *The Iceworker Sings*, supports the
publication of a first book by a Latino or Latina poet.
Awarded every other year, the prize is administered
by Letras Latinas–the literary program of the
Institute for Latino Studies
at the University of Notre Dame

The
Outer Bands

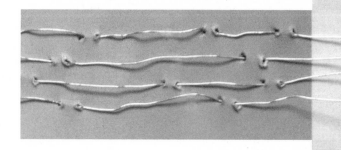

GABRIEL GOMEZ

University of Notre Dame Press

Notre Dame, Indiana

Published by the University of Notre Dame Press
Notre Dame, Indiana 46556
www.undpress.nd.edu

Designed by Wendy McMillen, type set in 9.8/14 Berthold Nofret
Printed on 55# Nature's Recycle Paper in the USA. by Versa Press

Library of Congress Cataloging-in-Publication Data
Gomez, Gabriel, 1973–
The outer bands / Gabriel Gomez.
p. cm. – (The Andrės Montoya Poetry Prize ; 2006)
ISBN-13: 978-0-268-02972-2 (pbk. : alk. paper)
ISBN-10: 0-268-02972-5 (pbk. : alk. paper)
I. Title.
PS3607.O488O98   2007
811'.6—dc22
                                        2007019490

For Julie

Contents

III

IV

Acknowledgments

Grateful acknowledgment to the editors of *580 Split* where "Cupola" and "This Particular Season" first appeared. Part IV: The Outer Bands includes headlines taken from the *New York Times*, August 30 to September 30, 2005. Much gratitude to Valerie Martínez for selecting these poems, The Santa Fe Art Institute and the Mills Writers Foundation–thank you for providing the space and funding to complete this book.

I also wish to thank my family Ernestina Gomez, Gilberto Gomez, Laura Gomez, and Gil Gomez. The Bernard family: Mary Elaine, Lewis, Charlene, Eddie, Angela, Juhye, John, and Jindallae. Maria Melendez for all her thoughtful commentary, advice, and friendship. Francisco Aragon for all his important work and devotion to poetry. Sheliah Wilson at SFAI and my fellow residents: Diane, Dave, Anne, Zach, Sandy, Michelle, Gordana, and Sharon. Thanks to Greg Glazner, a true mentor and teacher.

Jeremy, Karen, and Liam for the years of friendship, cold beer, use of their kitchen, and shelter from the storm. Henry, Kristen, and Gwen, thank you for the friendship, bonfires, broken bread, and off-color jokes. A very special thanks to Kate Ingold for her friendship and beautiful artwork created for the cover of this book. The City of New Orleans–life is still sweet. Calder–the best running partner a man could have.

And most importantly, all my love and appreciation to my most thoughtful reader Julie, who has held it down unconditionally through all of it–mi amor, mi alma, mi vida.

Joie de Vivre.

Introduction to the Poems

The importance of the Andrés Montoya Prize, beyond the recognition it gives to some of our best American poets, is the snapshot it provides of Latino poetry in the twenty-first century. The fifteen finalist manuscripts for 2006 show the range and richness and diversity of this body of work. There are lyric poets, narrative poets, meditative poets, rhetorical poets. There are urban and rural poets, traditional and experimental. There are manuscripts written in English and others that are bilingual by varying degrees.

Overall, the manuscripts show that Latino poets write not from one kind of experience but from the varied and particular experiences of this nation's large Latino community. This community is broad, embracing Chicanos, Cuban–Americans, Hispanics, Puerto Rican Americans, Mexican–Americans, Spanish immigrants, immigrants from Costa Rica, El Salvador, Honduras, and South America. This community extends from the tip of Florida to the northwest shorelines of Alaska. Our literature–Latino Literature, American Literature–defines us only as it collectively explores this enormous physical and cultural terrain.

At the same time, the best of these manuscripts embrace "culture"–the contemporary state of being that is "Latino." In one we might recognize "culture" in terms of landscape, historical allusion, and proper nouns. In another, biblical language and allusions to faith and prayer remind us of the deep roots of spirituality in our culture. In another, images of neighborhood, family, and childhood chronicle a personal past. But "culture" is never predictable, not simple and codified in a literary way. It is complex and contradictory, devout and heretical–layered, unpredictable, inclusive. Mestizo, mestiza–Latino.

This year's winner, *The Outer Bands* by Gabriel Gomez, is (perhaps above all) a wonderfully written collection that takes all sorts of risks. The first poem reads: "I'm telling you a story of brick and bone . . . I'm handling their images in my hand/a series of retablos." And each of the book's four sections defines the poetic "retablo" in different ways. Sometimes it is a short, lyric poem; sometimes it is a prose poem, and sometimes is both. Often the poems employ juxtaposition–encounters between different kinds of diction and form–to resonate with reflection and emotion. And the poems do the best of what I think contemporary American poetry is doing, employing quick leaps of syntax and association that are laden (not devoid) with resonance and meaning.

This is a book about language and landscape–how the poet exists in them, moves through them, and shivers with emotion and understanding. There are many riveting lines–"*a murder of crows dance like behemoth electrons*"; "there is no death nor myth, but crickets lumbering in patterns"; "because, as children, we have thought of the sun as an onion." Gabriel Gomez is an accomplished poet, one who honors the resonance of language as well as reverberations of form. And, like a retablo, each poem shimmers with reverence, if not for saints and biblical figures, then for the beauty and poignancy of complex, contemporary life.

The final section is a twenty-eight–part poem, an account of the early days in the aftermath of Hurricane Katrina, with dates and newspaper headlines followed by short provocative poems in different forms. Some locate us in the devastation of New Orleans; some tell us what's happening at the same moment somewhere else; some speak to us in the rhetoric of inept politicians. Gomez writes:

Tuesday, August 30, 2005

HURRICANE SLAMS INTO GULF COAST: DOZENS ARE DEAD

what I'm about to tell you is euphemism

and not unlike storytelling:

1. character development
2. primary conflict
3. symbolism
4. catharsis

Later we read: "the concrete   swept us / to the current // the virgin looked // like an oil stain // on a driveway." And then: "This is . . . a representation of my home."

This last poem is a moving account of the poet's own loss and displacement, the journey from the devastation of New Orleans to the Southwest and back. He chronicles the "savage movement of things," where "unrest was the least of it for now; our mouths and throats glowed into numbness as we ate." It is a testament to this poet's talent that Gomez is able to write about personal experience in a way that draws us deeper into the reality (visual and visceral) of a devastated American city while chronicling the political and social forces swirling in and around it.

It is my pleasure to introduce Gabriel Gomez and *The Outer Bands*. You will not be disappointed.

–Valerie Martínez,
Judge

The Outer Bands

I am alone among rickety substances

the rain falls upon me and it seems like me,

like me with its madness, alone in the dead world,

rejected as it falls, and without persistent shape

–Pablo Neruda

I

Cupola

I'm telling you a story of brick and bone,
of merciless rain subduing cars in their tracks.

I'm handling their images in my hand
a series of retablos,
haloed faces in vapored windows.

There is a picture of us sleeping,
dreaming through an entire evening
like nomads, twisted in the unembarrassed
lightness of our flesh at rest.
Our mouths agape in frozen postulate.
Our arms and legs uprooted.

This furious architecture,
this severed connection,
has forgotten the origin of you and I.
Buildings rise out of our arrested flesh.
Veins stunning along our arms
forgotten in our ambivalent embrace
between now and nowhere.

Coined

, spoke in foam soliloquy

to your
                    pierce–less ear.

Wading fog slept
            spooned with puzzled
                    sea
                    vine.

Hear it now? Brine copper light? A serpentine root?

Wind's gravity maybe.

A porous skin.
Stone jowl.

Bite, neigh, awake

for rain on yellowed root

How random.
                                An augur:
Shoulder flora milled after car breeze
Picasso's "Night Fishing at Antibes"

non–native grass

quelled

now sleeps . . .

Curriculum

The indifferent and the non-respondent. The edited and motion-less. Bounced from a plastic cup etched with a drift of pictured birds on a phosphoric seaside. You, let's say, will stop, drink, and find it necessary, ambivalent, and obviously musical to examine the knowledge of her against what is known about her. The urge to de-monize. To recall motive. Your thoughts wrapped and designated equally to describe what you were originally thinking. The previ-ous and subsequent billowing of blips above her head. The gears wasting no time and turning. For you, the sequence of her setting hair becomes standard and busy. Driven, dismantled, then gone to nothing being further from the truth. Her sizable image cones to disappearance. The entitlement of a harrowing sky. The walls and images of painted faces projecting a hum about you. Another ver-sion of you standing in the wonder of you, matter-less. The drinker, the wonder, the version, the will to shape the constant motion of it all–outfits a curriculum of all her faces into one.

Glaciers

November hardened the ocean with coral
tuna swim by
richness
iced darkness
dimmed to a stunning hue
a melody syncopated with dancing

now the desert

leaves   branches

root   canopy

mule deer   starlight

eroding coastline

the sea above

now the plains
mountains

where it used to thrive
spoken by layers

glacier to stone then tree

height   weight   design

inaudible for poetry

Lost in Translation

The kinship with those humans
who speak directly to me
is webbed to the ceiling.
An economy of satellites, a cosmos,
where revision we think
comes without the benefit
of our witness. A peculiar time
when stars with modest faces
sleep in enormity and mirror   .
death like a child's infirmity that
despite socio–economics
is still an illness,
definitive as fading paint
grossing a distant
understanding from a stain
pooled from its center
resonant of some terrific
nucleus making sense
of its own words
with the strangest electricity.

Over Night Low

There is sadness to this hard palisade. The same avenues

rise like ravines.   Its figurative whisper,

whispers.   Windows, if you will,

are fingerprints pressed into buildings of mud.

A river path on virgin   desert faces

smile through the concrete.

You and I are useless idolatry.

This Particular Season

The sensibilities in speech of winter

where process is undressed

of all history. The matter with fact

bankrupt theories to her blue dress

lifting in the crisp marina.

Here then are the engine plumes

living among us in a relative manner,

resemble breath proportion to appropriate capacity.

The ancient computer mothering in the hamlet sighs:

How old are you, then, when is it a good time

to call and dictate a list of imperatives for the lyric hero?

Remember the girl, once a projected form

dancing about the marina,

this particular season is pointing to her name.

A word that is easily rhymed then readily forgotten.

Timbre

I can't tell you I had climbed for hours on
ledges and crawled through gaps in the earth.

My hands negotiating
through the teeth of the palisade
lipped under the vineyard of temperate skies.

And I can't tell you that I came
onto a ledge within the shelter of a granite roof,
ceaselessly carved by centuries of dripping water.

Feeding from pooled water and singular sunlight
a chamisa plant sat like a chopped wood.

The opposite end of root
speaking for its entirety through
silence and color.

And I wish I could tell you that at the moment
I met its splitting scent under the enormity of stone
your name appeared in my throat with clarity.

And I wish we were old
and in front of a grand painting,
a picture or postcard of
Picasso's "Guernica" perhaps.
It would be then that I would tell you
Picasso once said that it took him his entire life
to learn how to paint like a child.

It would be through these words
that would make you understand
the same clarity that pooled over me
on that ledge those years before
when as a young man I extended
like direction, like timbre itself
for a dying song that echoed your name.

Crash

A woman wanders the scene of her crash–

Highway 84–64.   A wisp of pinion slurs the highway.

Prickling, engine, popping, asking

                              come in.

Wheels tossed in cool sand spin the emptiness forward.

A driver, stunned, walks, leans into the window flush with
ground.

Brocade of blood scoops her cheek.

She greets the company of strangers.

                         Call the ambulance.

A voice interrupts the trembling location.

Clean her face with dampened Kleenex.

Prickling, engine, popping, asking

Grammar schooled name   location answers

      Hold the ground against this fiction.

You've gone for good   the light is out.

Left hand over your mouth

speaks the distance traveled in volumes

A Slender Chemistry
of Wondrous Fiction

A concern for a crucifix fastened above a threshold.

A suspicion of rain in elderly bones.

These hold themselves in fragments,

standardized thinking.

I surround myself with hindsight of over turned earth

beside a paddock of whinnying foals; their wedged

hoofs chipping half-moons in the planks under dusk, where

there is no death nor myth, but crickets lumbering in patterns.

Their faces come apart like anthills in the rain.

Their smoldering voices pluming towards the darkness.

II

20 Retablos

The red scene begins with a swift sketch
A still life motivated from the instant flashing

Her hands warming in her pockets, re–balling tissue in a hard rhythm. Circling a name for her sun disturbed shadow of conch simplicity to an animated form spilling a ribbon of paths to the spearing sorghum. A final dust lifting under and after the weight of dew whispering the act of skin. Her name, I once recalled, meant unraveling in Spanish.

As with all parables there are four base colors

I learned that there is always food at the reckoning of a tragedy. Paint eagerly represents a woman as still life, diffused through hundreds of movements by her painter. Put trees through a window behind her; offer a texture circling of blue shadow stirring in pools of tea colored sand. Her name will come in a lipped octave slope saving the impulse to point at what you mean you'll want to say.

the hands were once attached to the arms
the face and legs have dropped to the imagination
the legs became deeper with marble
when rising toward the pinched waist

I learned to smoke behind the San Fernando church. We smoked *faros* that looked like joints, so we imagined that too. The church was named after a saint that had suffered patiently through a complicated and unreasonable death.

crops of lavender, shin height, plump with aroma
smeared the tillage with a tidy summary
the soil re-occurred for miles under the fashioned horizon
losing its light to the opposite page

there is distance in the drowning color
similitude to the shifty ochre light marching heavily upon us
the ocean kept re-occurring on the beach in the form of a wave

There were several interesting horizons.

because, as children, we have thought of the sun as an onion
we now remember its cells lifting from the rosy sepulcher
spilling in a wave, a repetitive signal
enouncing it coming to pummel the ground

The ground re–occurred through everything.

people surface towards the page
creatures pilot through a highway
their language is untranslatable
the road they carry is shaped
with a foreign math

the sunrise is a small child
the metaphor became easy to denounce
once it was known that there are no small
children depicted in heaven
the sun became an anterior math
an inconceivable exegesis

two objects clamor towards the specter

a woman squinting through the double sided mirror
a woman walking separately

as a child I was fascinated with powdered cement
diffused with so much water then hardened into form

the series returned deep swallow of sound and saliva

brown cardigan holding balls of tissue in their pockets
lifting and dropping

a pattern of gauzy shadows spilled from the giant red trees the fragrant moment of thirst

a curious and particular hunger
you mean for me to stay here
enter willingly

dew huddled on the stems of lilacs

like rock candy

a murder of crows dance like behemoth electrons

Humidity advanced thrillingly to her skin. The sharp gray sheets of rain dissipating slowly over the walkways and the cloistered verandas. Then an eventual puddle found your skin and lifted small dimples on your arms and neck. Over the mass of earth is the river, which all this traffic is under with an insoluble thirst

your back was neatly paragraphed by your blouse
I came around you like the movements of a flood

Doldrums jerked with fog
memory kept re-occurring
even from that place, where I had never been,
seemed natural to transplant every place
I'll call it media luna

my father kept semi precious rocks from Mexico in a lit cabinet resurrected artifacts of other peoples lives

there was another American who had married a Mestiza woman

he raised an indefinite number of pigs with his wife

his truck was dolphin blue

III

Map Reader

The arrival of stars.
The loop of asphalt in the twilight.
A peculiar bluff of windmills.
A headlamp pucker in the fog.
Everything left of Bakersfield.
A good map in color.
Grids, numbers, and things.
The steering wheel eating itself.
You think of a petroglyph.
The radio less than definitive,
stays on high.
The cold clap bark of metaphor
humming beneath you.
The sunlight that causes one to think simply.
Point and describe the going stars as wrinkled.

Adagio for Strings

As a boy, I walked the ruinous desert corridor
waiting for the rain.
Heeled cupped patterns
salted effigies like quantum stones
behind each step.

Years ago now,
an idea between valleys
like falling,
like cello extending
before an inconceivable void
separating before the body,
disparate arm leading,
then, stops, reconnects,
pools. Befalls new desert.

Rain, now, budding sand
where walking
sounds of eyelids
lifting to the oldest moment
of bodies,
lifting the other's weight
with breathing and tone of
repeating deluge
to awaken you
from what I thought
I was about to remember.

Inverness

We walked in the fat buckeyes, strung, plump violas, half nibbled by mule deer. The seismologist, the poet, and I reached our seats in the ox–blood Volvo wagon and rode away from Tomales Bay. The breeze still bit and I remembered the seismologist describe the coastline in literal terms as if a distressed woman had entered the car abruptly. The silence, analysis, and execution of thought, stressing the madness that lied beneath the surface of the lapping water.

The poet, I imagined, thought of lament or Orpheus for Eurydice. The torrent carving itself into an exhaustive note, ascending and descending onto its lonesome body, its flesh and bone indeterminate, transient, subjective of memory that will never doubt its truth.

"This place is capable of anything, infinitum," waxed the seismologist. "Como escribir, despues del infinito?" I answered. That's Spanish? he asked. Vallejo, I said. The poet still said nothing and drove us back to Inverness. I thought of telling him that as a boy, I had read his mediations on the roof of my parent's house, but didn't. I only stared at the back of his head as it moved over the unleveled asphalt towards his house.

The recyclables in the Volvo became a whirlwind in the switchbacks. We entered the house and began to gather our things. We were of course guests. On the way to the door, the poet stopped me and as he spoke, he handled a book of his poems in his hands like clay.

I wondered what I knew of this moment, but it didn't happen then. It happened now. And as it happened, you and I, were at the ocean and thought of Vallejo. How can we write when there is the infinite? Because it is the infinite, you replied.

Rebirth

The walls have hardly any filling: deadened plaster, wire, an inert flesh stirring blood (Jonah reclined on sticky walls, breathing a comfortable silent humidity). I'm its only texture in the cavity, but when I'm listening to these things through the walls, she is someone else entirely. These diminutive voices absorbed by the flesh throttle themselves from definition as if to gesture beyond their own crystal prisons. To feather and flight, an end is racing towards her from the sound.

There being no light, the void complete, whole belief and believability, body without arms, formless animas pitched within rich walls of silent stories, an open path set before the coming life.

This work begins almost immediately. Victorious dust gathering for bone, minuet spine, nerve sloughs, skin becomes wall. Slight drips skirt her face. I assembled her two arms twisted from the shoulder, raised them out of the bulb darkness and drank.

It's a building room, reawakened with old light, vinegar doused windows, other baptisms, and so it goes. The flesh resurrects, houses breath and voice. Floating bodies are unlike memories in any arrangement, but to hear these voices and to witness their reaction is a life already unraveling.

Paper

a wind riffles through milk thistle

endemic with path

moves   indiscriminately   turns

a furious knot of kinky hair

to something more alive and unclean

but in the kindest moment

exposes leaf

Figurines

You turn to realize the statement that explains the brushstroke, a like-ness, explains a veiled face. An inky gaze beyond an alphabet of another likeness. Memory happened in contrast to the story one thought re-verses to before sentence. Before one could describe the road smoking after rain, the asphalt as avalanche. The seriousness is endless and suggests a woman's body lured in mobility—perhaps in the oldest bar in town where anything is probable. Her hair awakens as if in the strands ran blood. The eye emits color from the concentrated circle. Smoke clouds are silver petals gashing like pouting lips or slender arms in contrast to aspen trunks. Her concentric sigh lifting from the page. Words themselves pointing meagerly. The troublesome music ends abruptly. Lights on. Her dress once tethered clumsily in your arms turns into the fragrance of sentences.

Bluegrass

I.

sound knots

pinned to a fabric–less body form of oak bone

a barreled chest

the presence of acoustic music over the instrument

resting on your lap

a limited vehicle   but you knew that

having learned tablature

the guitar posed in sculpture

clear its throat by reaching the oval gap flushed

against stomach into its curious sound

gather fingers around an inexhaustible voice and play the strings

II.

bread shaped to song as we ate and fidgeted

the pitch of river
frozen to stillness   a film
reeled and taut

swelling water
oily in its cold
steps before it hardens

an utterance before song is shaped

a compression of freezing water
eating away at its own babbling face

III.

where are the boxes of clothes

the newspaper to scoop inside of cups

feel free to comment

miss nothing as of chewing a new food

these are features of comfort

a lower altitude,

moved further but   no egg crate to snug the ends of the hutch

a chimera of tempered sand

speak of her house absolved by the wiping ocean

speak of her name by way of mountains

the mirrors   silver flaking for the edges of the mirrors

leaving only glass   unreflective patches

the promised half

the unanswerable ruin of aperture   begging

from where you haven't seen yourself in years

Lebanon, Tennessee

"I know if I was in Mexico I would make an effort to learn Hispanic."
–Bob Bright, 61, Insurance Agent, Lebanon, Tennessee

this is as you were before the sentence
crossed your sculpted oak parapet
before moving in the hollows of marble hallways
a gallery of chambers filled with human movement
Oaxacan legs scissoring towards a courthouse in Lebanon Tennessee

I had heard of you before we'd even arrived; I didn't need to read
You looked like that panzon chicarronero that would give us torrejitas to lift our skirts
I was cold; my arms folded over my belly; my hands burned from clorox
The room was clean like a hospital
What were you thinking when you imagined me on my back?

here to learn English and resist having children.
excise the very meaning and symbol, the childhood simulacra of earthen
bone and thigh exacted with boundaries
a reasonable logical comatose symbol

We were less than ourselves
Like segments of Mixteco
Wintry moorings and polished bones of lost Novembers.
But here in my hand, the smear of shit and blood
From dismantled hens turns the earth to salt

the inlet
the ivory foam cooing hollow bays
lift and behold our map
the pronounced air vacillates between lives
rise and the aimless feeling is gone

Murmation of Starlings

Now and again, in the stone element
a murmation of starlings swaddle themselves through
wintry mornings. Their plaintive swoops abound
with murmur and singularity in the sunlit breeches.

We, I realized, must roam stupidly to them.

Instinct overcomes the diminutive scapula.
What luck to have found them
so dumb and simply

where one represents the body
the other crests and bows

the image
still as glass
concurs

The dynamic sound that is

Learning to move discreetly through the empty morning hallways

listening to the wind boring the intricate pitch of senseless walls

redolent sound chambered like drilling

I enter it

the dynamic sound that is

an emergent surge for answers

bubbles densely within the throat

acidic queries tumble to the young and vacuous wonder of early days

and I remember

the sudden rising of buildings, of ourselves

once an intricate mud, split from bastion of bottomless ejido

to a wedged horizon wasted by a porous drift

of the returning brood

skin   white as darkness

IV

The Outer Bands

HURRICANE SLAMS INTO GULF COAST; DOZENS ARE DEAD

what I'm about to tell you is euphemism

and not unlike story telling

1. character development
2. primary conflict
3. symbolism
4. catharsis

the placement of ordinary things

Wednesday, August 31, 2005

NEW ORLEANS IS INUNDATED AS 2 LEVEES FAIL; MUCH OF GULF COAST IS CRIPPLED; TOLL RISES

new canyons   lift

            from carving water   the city stands

            here

walls
lift

    from the ground

like carapace   arch and pitch of sepia fiords

              wandering

and

    exposed

THE SUPERDOME
At Stadium, a Haven Quickly Becomes an Ordeal

CHICAGO, IL: At the Sears Tower, two young Amish couples wait with us in the lobby as it filled steadily. Rows of elevators for the Sky Deck flanked the gauntlet of guard rails, commemorative photo stations, and fifty cent imprint penny smashers. $11.95 for adults just to look. Each elevator was chicken–bus packed. Ears popped as we rose. The boy's firm suspenders wedged into their soft backs. Their black straw, pork–pie style hats framed trimmed hair. Bonnet shaped the girl's delicate skull.

Her beautiful profile approached and smiled when her hand touched the cool glass–tracing the light of Wisconsin, Michigan, Indiana–the angled Chicago palisade outlined by her extended finger.

Because we note the entirety at once
the piece and sum are one.

DESPAIR AND LAWLESSNESS GRIP NEW ORLEANS AS THOUSANDS REMAIN STRANDED IN SQUALOR
Local Officials Criticize Federal Government Over Response

CHICAGO, IL: Day Two

obscure sound

waves moistened

our chapped skin

highway fell
curiously

on
pungent combustion

the concrete   swept us
to the current

the virgin looked

like an oil stain

on a driveway

MORE TROOPS AND AID REACH NEW ORLEANS:
BUSH VISITS AREA: CHAOTIC EXODUS CONTINUES
Conditions in City Still Dire: Pumping May Take Months

she showed me the quarry

where stone had been measured

exacted   from the larger body of stone

    she showed me

    the photograph of her father

he wore a uniform

stood with broad shoulders

into the lens

        she made me guess which one he was

the slow carved frame cupped his image

her face exacted from his like quarried stone

Paul, I said, when I touched the glass

56

BUSH PROMISES MORE TROOPS AS
NEW ORLEANS QUIETS
Evacuations Increasing with Guard on Patrol and Offering Aid

imagine

the sleeping stranger   awakening

        finding sleep   too incongruous

      enumerate   R.   E.   M.

                    erupts

                    heaves

                    swells

bronzed tempera leaves in its wake

white paper dissipates   like behemoth confetti   in the brackish dew

Monday, September 5, 2005

NEW ORLEANS BEGINS A SEARCH FOR ITS DEAD
Toll Remains Unclear – 20 States to Give Aid and Housing

a new dust   oyster shell   discovered on the

mountain

settled loons turned   thick opaque eyes   their throats in mournful

thirst

marveled   the evaporating sea

peaks appeared

black plumage   white belly

sinewy lichen
unearthed

piercing wails   exit the wilderness

aghast at the light

lift their winter crowns

Tuesday, September 6, 2005

STORM AND CRISIS: IMMIGRANTS
Double Trap for Foreign Workers

we talked about black mold with indoor voices
incapable hands adjusting insurance

news of places looted or abandoned for good
polite and mechanical translations

the embarrassment of handling
soaking books and clothes to the street

never spoken

ubiquitous splinters   a waft of ruined air   nude of humidity

a nuance in guilt expressed

                              didn't have it quite as bad
                              mere wind damage

the used sofa
purchased with borrowed money
four years ago now ruined

you and I are the new saints from similar frequencies
an erupting clutch of common flicker coming to rest

FLOODING RECEDES IN NEW ORLEANS; US INQUIRY IS SET
Pressure on Holdouts Grows – Fear of Fire and Disease

a study in deprivations

reward for the

less involved

this is the idea

of being away

from something

FORCED EVACUATIONS OF A BATTERED
NEW ORLEANS BEGINS
Officials Warn of Disease and Fire Risks

driving through Texas

for the third time in a month

we stopped outside Dallas

south becomes pin-prick

"F" in sign language

clear of sea level

streets no longer peppered

with chalky dry wall

river silt

nails to puncture tires

restaurants without rice

in their salt shakers

a less pliable air
a lesser sun

                  humidity escapes

                  the skin in the desert

                  until it cracks, peels, and splits

                  from our lips

                  like boiling cinnamon

COST OF RECOVERY SURGES, AS DO BIDS TO JOIN IN EFFORT
Experts Put Government's Tab at More Than $100 Million

we met for beers in El Paso

he told us about living in Brazil

with his wealthy ex-girlfriend

who graduated

from an expensive art school

in New York

                    her most poignant ideas are mine he said

DIRECTOR OF FEMA STRIPPED OF ROLE AS LEADER
Decision comes after lawmakers put pressure on president

SANTA FE, NM:

slept like the dead in Liam's nursery

bundles of cloth diapers

stacked like ammunition

in a bunker

the accruements of childbearing

stain resistant swaddling blankets

fuzzy bunz diaper wrappers

ergonomically designed diaper bags / hiking rebozo

and so on

Breakdowns marked path from
hurricane to anarchy
In crisis, federal authorities hesitated – local officials were overwhelmed

SANTA FE, NM: Attended pet parade; it looped through downtown and into the plaza; children walked their pet rabbits, strapped afro wigs on Dobermans, and bent romex wiring into chicken feet for laughs; things I consider innocent, simple, and ironic as I consider sunlight innocent, simple, and ironic. Girls twirled batons and flipped; boys played instruments; Elvis karate chops to "who let the dogs out." We followed the last of the humiliated pets onto the plaza. Spontaneous strophe, "que viva la fiesta"; antistrophe "viva!" Casual shoppers grunted; pawed the beaten silver.

Coastal Cities of Mississippi in the Shadows:
Area Faces Aftermath Out of Media Glare
BUSH GOES BACK TO NEW ORLEANS
FOR INSPECTION

SANTA FE, NM: Drank for several hours atop the La Fonda hotel at a bar we never knew existed. Coming from below sea level the drinks were considerably effective. I imagined the syntax of my speech turning into an Art Blakey drum roll compounded with expletives and something like honking. The men and women around the bar were familiar; these were the same tourists I had seen seven years ago when I left for grad school; these are also the same people in the Quarter hamming it for sharpie caricatures of themselves atop Mt. Everest. The same fanny pack, comfortable white shoes, and affection for video taping immobile architecture; I imagined the women at home tilling the mums with the fleur de lis spades and using words like "classy" when referring to restaurants they had visited.

The sunset was red.

45 Bodies Found in a New Orleans Hospital
Some victims are said to have died while awaiting rescue

one labored breath
comes from her mouth

    it appears

a moment gauzed   her father dismantled

against blue cold   still lingers

laurels tumble like bells   cease and huddle

against the ground   cornered until spring

PRESIDENT SAYS HE'S RESPONSIBLE IN STORM
LAPSES; PROBLEMS AT ALL LEVELS
He cites readiness to react to major terror attack

sitting in the exit row en route to Chicago

was asked to assist the crew in case of emergency

this too will go on my resume

Ex-FEMA Chief Tells of Frustration and Chaos

our water–

logged floor

bows like a sedge

of resting cranes

walls will

eventually burst

to the street

Bush Pledges Federal Role in Rebuilding Gulf Coast
Gives Speech in Heart of an Empty City

Index of Logical Fallacies: Excerpts from "Do What It Takes" A speech by President Bush, September 15, 2005: Jackson Square, New Orleans, LA

From Ignorance: Many of the men and women of the Coast Guard, the Federal Emergency Management Agency, the United States military, the National Guard, Homeland Security, and state and local governments performed skillfully under the worst conditions

Slippery Slope: Congress is preparing an investigation, and I will work with members of both parties to make sure this effort is thorough

Complex Question: In a time of terror threats and weapons of mass destruction, the danger to our citizens reaches much wider than a fault line or a flood plain

Appeal to Force: Americans have never left our destiny to the whims of nature, and we will not start now

Appeal to Pity: Armies of compassion, charities and houses of worship and idealistic men and women that give our reconstruction effort its humanity

Prejudicial Language: They remind us of a hope beyond all pain and death–a God who welcomes the lost to a house not made with hands

Stating the Obvious: There is also some deep, persistent poverty in this region as well. And that poverty has roots in a history of racial discrimination, which cut off generations from the opportunity of America

Anonymous Authority: I will listen to good ideas from Congress

Style over Substance: wounded healers

False Analogy: We are the heirs of men and women who lived through those first terrible winters at Jamestown and Plymouth, who rebuilt Chicago after a great fire, and San Francisco after a great earthquake, who reclaimed the prairie from the dust bowl of the 1930s

Slothful Induction: In addition, we are taking steps to ensure that evacuees don't have to travel great distances or navigate bureaucracies to get the benefits that are there for them

Inconsistency: taxpayers expect this work to be done honestly and wisely, so we will have a team of inspector generals reviewing all expenditures

Hasty Generalization: Thank you, and may God bless America

FEMA, Slow to the Rescue,
Now Stumbles in Aid Effort
Officials and Evacuees Tell of Frustration with Poorly Coordinated Recovery

a new mountain appeared

        oaks laid unremarkably

        like broken saxophones   Julie snapped photos

from the car
for friends

aghast   in the new and silent image

the shutter

punched the air

methodically

BUSINESS OWNERS START TO RETURN TO
NEW ORLEANS
STRICT CURFEW ENFORCED

Nearby parish residents come home to little power or water

the body betrays the spirit in a cancerous architecture

Vulnerable, and Doomed in the Storm, 154 Died in Hospitals and Nursing Homes as Rescue Lagged

where the marching birds sat together

book cases lifted in the rising water

an index of spines

falling toward the floor

pages fasten to the wood

eves from slick
gluey pages

like advertisements on plywood

aborted from their perch

swollen feathers hiding claws

expired   blossomed

in the grip of the trembling pool

MAYOR SUSPENDS FLOW OF PEOPLE TO
NEW ORLEANS
REVERSAL AFTER PRESSURE
He Calls for Evacuation, Citing New Storm and Weakened Levees

the city still slept without an eye to the world

its child watching the parent sob into its hands

the susceptible image put away

be on fire

says the memory of what's come about

the grown man remembers the
moment as unexpectedly real

STORM AND CRISIS: THE DEFENSES
Design Flaws Seen in New Orleans Flood Walls

the lifting body suggests unconsciously

leg
torso
thighs   evenly balanced

running too begins with the legs

small collapse   of bone   to cartilage

sinewy
lurch

why connect them and with what   awakened from hard sleep

breathing bodies   inflate   collapse

like buoys

feet extended   fill again

with blood

76

hobbling first steps until

the long gallop

      makes dynamic bodies
                    cities disappear into nowhere at once

STORM AND CRISIS: THE OVERVIEW
GULF HURRICANE OF TOP STRENGTH MENACES TEXAS

Julie's Birthday. Music began behind the disheveled voices; rectangles of paint coursed like ground water. Men walked over guitars; spoke through the corners of their mouths while eyeing the line and curvature of moving women. Every vicarious soul in the room was mere correspondence of something less dramatic; an armoire of tattered clothes and footprints where everyone has stepped. We were talking about the media and the simile of war, "See, this did not exist for anyone who was not there," said my friend. The milky-way was evident through the skylight and the desert seemed pliable, full of promise and order under its caption of evening light. Before, the sunset had been transmutable; futility in reproducing the color for canvas. We were lost on the way there; the directions assumed too much. The clerk at the Allsup's wore a beige polo shirt with his name and the name of local hotel embroidered on his chest. Bill seemed annoyed by my questions.

STORM AND CRISIS: NEW ORLEANS;
Shift in Storm's Path Raises Fears About Weak New Orleans Levees

what I'm about to tell you

is that there is plenty

of self-storage in Lafayette Louisiana

dotting the segmented pasture

more acreage than nature

like a pilled sweater

imagine the stackable plastic bins

resting in sheet metal bunker

letters

porcelain dolls

household imagery   filling

translucent boxes like x-rayed intestines

STORM AND CRISIS: TRAFFIC DEATHS;
Bus Evacuating Senior Center Burns, Killing 24 Near Dallas

Hurricane Katrina Disaster Relief and Economic Recovery Act

Protecting Essential Louisiana Infrastructure, Citizens, and Nature
Commission (PELICAN)

Louisiana Recovery Authority

Louisiana Recovery Corporation

Bring New Orleans Back Commission

Rebuilding Louisiana Coalition

Louisiana Economic Development

Gulf Opportunity Zone

Worker Recovery Accounts

People's Hurricane Relief Fund and Oversight Coalition

Urban Homesteading Act

STORM AND CRISIS: THE OVERVIEW;
HURRICANE SLAMS INTO GULF COAST; FLOODING SPREADS

in the savage movement of things
the wandering ideal
collects inside the naked happiness
of feeling nothing for the thing
a lifetime filled with renting
waiting in line
living indoors

the end comes before compartments
are leveraged
before the black and bludgeoned
face on Bourbon Street
has us to deal with
before splendor
rebirth
the smell of low–tide

after the city now refused to awaken

Postscript: The Cost of Recovery

The bar only serves beer and feigned Creole delicacies: fried shrimp, oyster shooters, something called gator sauce, and of course Buffalo wings with varying degrees of spice, presumably designed to be extinguished by the accompanied beer specials. The bartender had her breasts cinched up to her neck and exposed a diminutive waist punctuated by alarmingly prevalent hip bones and a moon shaped navel ring. She smiled deeply, almost querulous, without absence.

We waited for our buffalo wings in the closeted dark of Crawdaddy's Tavern. This is where many hours had been spent during my early twenties while home from school. I explained to Julie how I was expelled from the local university my freshmen year for sleeping with my "wonders in algebra" professor and how as a teenager I inhaled my first lung full of weed from a dented Dr. Pepper can at a church retreat. You lie, Julie said.

We found ourselves here in the bosom of a faux–Acadiana–32 days after Hurricane Katrina among the insidious bayou posters and images, emblematic charlatans, and exotic–ized Cajun kitsch like the mural which consumed half the wall: an alligator ladling gumbo from a cauldron while sipping on a cocktail. This is the ancillary market of New Orleans and a representation of my home. The Americana of mid–western porcelain masks, over–weight and beaded denizens hiding embossed conference logos, and drinking hand grenades, hurricanes, Abita beer. The competing image of the flood. The free radical informing the cancer.

For us, it is respite. A slight pathos of home where pieces of my youth and behavior flood every cell, every sinewy. Where I attempt to amuse Julie with a history of my fuck-ups, reminding her that we have each other. The charlatan. The stage. The façade. I worried for her until it burned, until our food arrived. Her face, fear, unrest was the least of it for now; our mouths and throats glowed into numbness as we ate.

GABRIEL GOMEZ

is a poet, playwright, and music journalist
born and raised in El Paso, TX.
He received a BA in Creative Writing
from the College of Santa Fe
and an MFA in Creative Writing
from St. Mary's College of California.
He has taught English at
the University of New Orleans,
Tulane University, the College of Santa Fe,
and the Institute of American Indian Arts.
He lives in Santa Fe, NM
with his wife Julie.